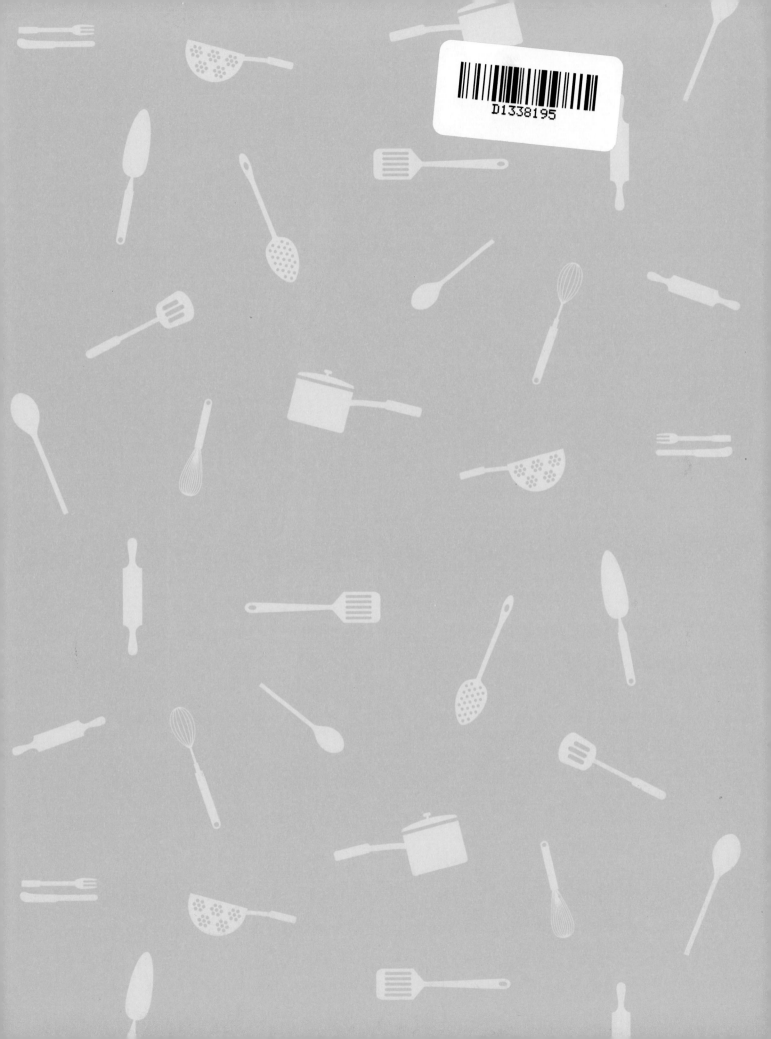

THE GREAT BRITISH
AFTERNOON TEA
COOKBOOK

BY NANCY LAMBERT

Licensed exclusively to Top That Publishing Ltd
Tide Mill Way, Woodbridge, Suffolk, IP12 1AP, UK
www.topthatpublishing.com
Copyright © 2016 Tide Mill Media
All rights reserved
0 2 4 6 8 9 7 5 3 1
Manufactured in China

CONTENTS

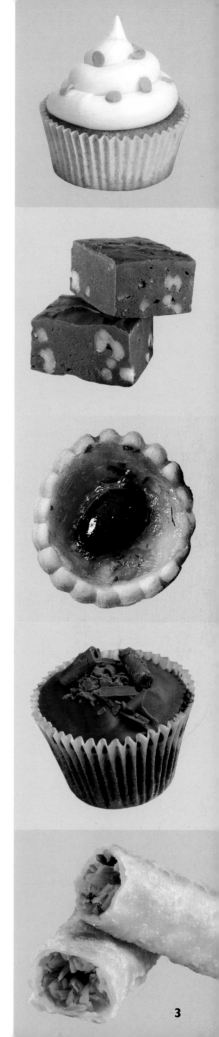

INTRODUCTION

From tea at London's famous Savoy Hotel to the Mad Hatter's everlasting tea party in Alice in Wonderland, what could be more British than afternoon tea? A fresh pot of piping-hot tea with dainty sandwiches, tantalizing savouries, irresistible cakes and other sweet treats … bliss!

When tea first arrived in Britain, in the 1650s, only royalty and the super-rich could afford to drink it. Luckily, this changed over time, and tea became the popular drink it is today.

We have the Duchess of Bedford to thank for afternoon tea. In early Victorian times 'dinner' was eaten around 7:30 to 8 pm. This was too long for the hungry Duchess to wait, so she started having her tea things brought to her room at five o'clock. And the rest, as they say, is history!

Now you too can become part of a great tradition and create delicious selections of teatime treats. Simply mix and match the tasty recipes in this book to design endless menus to delight your family and friends. Tea, anyone?

COOKING TIPS!

- Make sure you use the freshest ingredients available.

- Prepare all the food that you can in advance.

- If you are having tea outside, don't leave food for too long before it's eaten. Throw away any food that has been out for more than four hours.

- Remember that presentation is a big part of afternoon tea. Pretty china, crisp napkins, shiny cutlery, even flowers … go to town and make teatime a real event.

EQUIPMENT

- To complete the recipes in this book, you will need to use a selection of everyday cooking equipment and utensils, such as mixing bowls, saucepans, a sieve, knives, spoons and forks and a chopping board.

- Of course, you'll need to weigh and measure the ingredients, so you'll need a measuring jug and some kitchen scales too.

- To make some of the recipes in this book, you'll need to use special kitchen equipment such as a food processor. You'll find details in the recipes where necessary.

(Always read each recipe, in full, before buying ingredients and getting started!)

SAFETY & HYGIENE

- Before starting any cooking always wash your hands.

- Cover any cuts with a plaster.

- Wear an apron to protect your clothes.

- Always make sure that all the equipment you use is clean.

- If you need to use a sharp knife to cut up something hard, ask an adult to help you. Always use a chopping board.

- Remember that trays in the oven and pans on the cooker can get very hot. Always ask an adult to turn on the oven and to get things in and out of the oven for you.

- Always ask an adult for help if you are using anything electrical – like an electric whisk.

- Be careful when heating anything in a pan on top of the cooker. Keep the handle turned to one side to avoid accidentally knocking the pan.

- Keep your pets out of the kitchen while cooking.

**ADULT SUPERVISION
IS REQUIRED
FOR ALL RECIPES**

GETTING STARTED

MEASURING

Use scales to weigh exactly how much of each ingredient you need or use a measuring jug to measure liquids.

MIXING

Use a spoon, balloon whisk or electric hand whisk to mix the ingredients together.

CREATING RECIPES

Once you've made a recipe in this book a few times, think about whether you could make your own version. Don't be afraid to experiment with the recipes to find something you like. Try to think up names for the things you create!

PLEASE NOTE

The temperatures and measurements given in this book are approximate. Use the same measurement conversions throughout your recipe (grams or ounces) to maintain the correct ratios. All of the recipes in this book have been created for adults to make with junior chefs and must not be attempted by an unsupervised child.

Read through each recipe to make sure you've got all the ingredients and equipment that you need before you start.

ORCHARD TEA

Ingredients:

- 150 ml (5 fl.oz) boiling water
- 1 teaspoon Darjeeling tea
- 150 ml (5 fl.oz) apple juice
- 1 apple

This refreshing drink matches the sweetness of apple juice with the delicate taste of Darjeeling tea. Darjeeling tea is famous for its light golden colour and floral aroma. For best results make sure you don't over-brew Darjeeling. Tea bags take less time to brew than loose leaf tea.

1   Boil the water and pour over the tea.

2   Brew the Darjeeling for 3-5 minutes, and strain.

3   Add the apple juice and heat in a pan, but do not boil.

4   Serve hot in cups, with apple slices.

TOP TIP! Try serving this tea with apple and cinnamon cupcakes (see page 32).

SUMMER TEA

Ingredients:

• 500 ml (17 fl.oz) boiling water
• 5 teaspoons Assam tea
• 60 g (2 oz) sugar
• 375 ml (12½ fl.oz) orange juice
• 60 g (2 oz) strawberries, chopped
• mint, to decorate
• ice

Perfect for a hot afternoon in the garden, summer tea is a cooling drink for those days when you just want to chill. The orange juice helps cut through the strong taste of the Assam tea. This is a great drink to match with the garden cupcakes on page 54!

1 Boil the water and pour over the tea.

2 Brew for 3-5 minutes and then strain.

3 Add the sugar and orange juice and leave to cool in the fridge.

4 Divide the ice and chopped strawberries into tall glasses.

5 Add the cooled tea, and garnish with a sprig of mint to serve.

TOP TIP!
Why not experiment with other fruits?

11

APRICOT SAMOVAR TEA

SERVES 1

Ingredients:
- 250 ml (8½ fl.oz) boiling water
- 1 teaspoon strong black tea
- 1 tablespoon apricot jam, or other favourite jam
- dark sugar to taste
- cream (optional)

Tea isn't just an important drink in Britain; this gorgeous apricot tea is a classic Russian drink. A 'samovar' is a sort of Russian kettle, and a really important part of Russian tea culture. If you don't have apricot jam, you can try any other sweet jam.

1 Boil the water and pour over the tea.

2 Brew the tea; 3 minutes should be plenty.

3 Add the fruit jam and sugar.

4 Stir well, and add cream if you wish.

TOP TIP!
The Russian way to serve this drink is to put the jam on your tongue, then drink the tea black. This way you can taste the bitterness of the tea and the sweetness of the jam together!

HALA KAHIKI TEA

SERVES 6

Ingredients:
- 600 ml (20 fl.oz) boiling water
- 4 teaspoons loose tea
- 2 tablespoons mint leaves
- 600 ml (20 fl.oz) cold water
- 1 teaspoon lemon juice
- 100 g (3½ oz) sugar
- 125 ml (4 fl.oz) pineapple juice
- fresh pineapple to garnish

'Hala kahiki' is actually the Hawaiian name for the pineapple that is one of the key ingredients in this delicious teatime drink. Don't be scared of increasing the quantities; everyone is sure to want more than one glass, and it will safely keep in the fridge for a day.

1 Place the mint and tea in a pan, and pour on boiling water.

2 Cover and allow to brew for 5 minutes.

3 Strain the brewed tea into a jug containing the cold water.

4 Add lemon juice, pineapple juice, and sugar.

5 Pour into glasses over ice. Garnish with mint and pineapple pieces.

TOP TIP! This fruity tea is a great party drink!

13

PICK & MIX SANDWICHES

TOP TIP!
Separate the sandwiches if you know that there are vegetarians coming to the party.

MAKES 12

Ingredients:

- 6 slices of bread
- butter

For the fillings:

Cheese, Ham and Tomato

- 50 g (2 oz) cheddar cheese
- 2 slices of ham
- 1 large tomato, sliced

Egg Mayonnaise

- 1 egg
- 2 tablespoons mayonnaise
- salad (optional)

Chicken and Tomato

- 1/2 tomato
- 50 g (2 oz) cooked chicken
- salad (optional)

First, spread the butter on one side of each of the slices of bread. Next, start to layer up the filling insides.

Cheese, Ham and Tomato

Ask an adult to help you slice or grate the cheese. Place the cheese on one of the pieces of bread, followed by the ham. Add sliced tomato. Place another slice of bread on top and cut into four triangles.

Egg Mayonnaise

Place the egg in a saucepan half-filled with cold water and ask an adult to bring the water to a boil. Once the water is boiling, turn the heat down and let the egg simmer for about 7 minutes. When the egg has cooked, ask an adult to remove it from the hot water and let it cool. Carefully peel the shell off, then chop the egg into chunks. Put the egg chunks into a bowl and mix together with the mayonnaise. Spoon onto one of the pieces of bread. Add salad if you wish. Place another slice of bread on top and cut into four triangles.

Chicken and Tomato

Ask an adult to slice the tomato. Then, place the cooked chicken on one of the pieces of bread, followed by a couple of slices of tomato. Add salad if you wish. Place another slice of bread on top and cut into four triangles.

WRAP SANDWICHES

Ingredients:

• 8 flour tortilla wraps
• 4 tablespoons mayonnaise
• 4 slices of ham
• 50 g (2 oz) cheddar cheese, sliced
• 50 g (2 oz) green salad
• 2 large tomatoes, sliced
• 25 g (1 oz) cucumber, sliced
• 50 g (2 oz) cooked chicken, chopped

1 Place the tortillas on a work surface and spread each one with mayonnaise.

2 Divide the filling among the tortillas and then roll up tightly.

3 Cut each rolled tortilla into 5 cm (2 in.) sections.

4 Serve on a brightly coloured plate and watch them all disappear!

TOP TIP!
Experiment with different ingredients to create your favourite!

BRUSCHETTA BITES

Ingredients:
- half a baguette
- 4 tablespoons olive oil
- 8 large tomatoes
- basil leaves to garnish (optional)
- black pepper (optional)

1 Preheat the oven to 150°C / 325°F / gas mark 3.

2 Ask an adult to cut the baguette into about 12 (1.5 cm / 1/2 in.) thick slices and discard the end pieces. Place the slices on a large baking tray.

3 Drizzle half of the olive oil over the top side of the bread, turn over the slices and drizzle with the remaining oil.

4 Bake the bread for 10 minutes until it is golden and crisp. Ask an adult to remove it from the oven and cool slightly.

5 Meanwhile, ask an adult to chop up the tomatoes and place into a bowl.

6 Once cool, arrange the bruschetta on a serving platter and then top each with the chopped tomatoes.

7 Finally decorate with basil leaves and a sprinkling of black pepper, if desired.

TOP TIP!
Try rubbing a cut piece of garlic on the baked bread before adding the tomatoes!

PERFECT PANINIS

MAKES 2

Ingredients:

Red Pepper and Brie
- 1 panini roll
- 2 tablespoons mayonnaise
- 3 pieces roasted red pepper, fresh or from a jar
- 50 g (2 oz) brie, cut into slices
- a few lettuce leaves
- fresh herbs of your choice

Ham and Cheese
- 1 panini roll
- 2 tablespoons mayonnaise
- 50 g (2 oz) thinly sliced ham
- 25 g (1 oz) cheddar cheese, sliced

Preheat the grill to a medium heat, then preheat the oven to 180°C / 350°F / gas mark 4.

Red Pepper and Brie

1. Ask an adult to halve the panini with a sharp knife and toast both sides under a hot grill. Next, spread the cut sides with mayonnaise.

2. Arrange the pepper pieces on top of the mayonnaise-coated base. Top with brie.

3. Add a few small lettuce leaves and sandwich together with the top of the panini.

4. Finally, wrap the panini in foil and ask an adult to place on a baking tray in a preheated oven for 15 minutes.

5. Garnish with a freshly chopped herb of your choice and serve with salad!

Ham and Cheese

1. Prepare the panini as before, but instead, arrange the ham and cheese on top of the mayonnaise-coated base.

2. Sandwich together with the top of the panini and ask an adult to place into the oven to warm.

3. Serve with salad!

17

MINI FRITTATA

Ingredients:
- olive oil
- 50 g (2 oz) spring onions, sliced
- 100 g (3½ oz) red pepper, chopped
- 1 teaspoon dried oregano
- 200 g (7 oz) potatoes, cooked and chopped
- 8 eggs
- 100 g (3½ oz) cheddar cheese, grated

1 Preheat the oven to 200°C / 400°F / gas mark 6. Grease a non-stick 12-hole muffin tray with oil.

2 Ask an adult to heat some oil in a pan, and then add the onions, red pepper and oregano. Cook for a few minutes until tender and golden.

3 Then stir in the cooked potato and leave to cool.

4 Meanwhile, break the eggs into a jug, whisk and stir in the cheese.

5 Divide the vegetable mixture between the muffin tray holes and pour the egg and cheese mixture on top.

6 Bake for 15 mins until puffed, golden and set. Leave to cool slightly then pop out of the tray.

7 Cut the frittatas into bite-sized pieces or leave them whole.

TOP TIP!
Add chopped ham to this recipe in step 2 for party carnivores!

18

SAUSAGE BITES

Ingredients:

- 1 thin French stick
- 100 g (3½ oz) spicy sausage, i.e. chorizo
- 75 g (3 oz) cheddar cheese
- 1 green pepper
- butter or margarine to spread

1 First, ask an adult to cut the French stick into small bite-sized slices.

2 Now slice the spicy sausage and cheese into small pieces.

3 Wash the green pepper and then chop into small chunks also.

4 Spread a little butter or margarine onto each bread slice.

5 Then, start to build up the bites. Place a sausage slice on top of the bread, followed by a cube of cheese and finally a piece of pepper. Use a cocktail stick to hold each bite in place.

6 Repeat until the remaining ingredients have been used up.

TOP TIP!
If you're not a fan of spicy food, use any other kind of meat, or even veggie sausage instead!

19

CHEESE SCONES

Ingredients:

- 225 g (7 oz) self-raising flour
- pinch of salt
- 50 g (2 oz) butter
- 25 g (1 oz) mature cheddar cheese, grated
- 150 ml (5 fl.oz) milk

1. Preheat the oven to 200°C / 400°F / gas mark 6. Lightly grease a baking tray.

2. Mix together the flour and salt and rub in the butter.

3. Stir in the cheese, followed by the milk, to create a soft dough.

4. Knead the dough on a floured work surface. Then, roll out the dough until it is 2 cm (3/4 in.) thick.

5. Then, use a pastry cutter to cut out the scones and place them onto the baking tray. Brush the top of each scone with a little milk.

6. Ask an adult to place them into the preheated oven and bake for 12–15 minutes or until they have risen and are a nice golden colour.

7. Transfer the scones onto a wire rack and allow to cool.

TOP TIP!
Serve the scones with butter curls.

SPRING ROLLS

Ingredients:

- 50 g (2 oz) grated carrot
- 50 g (2 oz) tinned cannellini beans, rinsed
- 50 g (2 oz) fresh bean sprouts, chopped
- 1 spring onion
- 25 g (1 oz) mushrooms
- 1 tablespoon chilli dipping sauce
- 50 g (2 oz) cooked chicken, chopped
- vegetable oil
- 8 sheets square-shaped filo pastry

1   Preheat the oven to 200°C / 400°F / gas mark 6.

2   Put the grated carrot, beans and bean sprouts into a bowl and mix together well. Ask an adult to chop the spring onion and mushrooms into small pieces. Add these to the carrot, beans and bean sprouts and mix. Stir in 1 tablespoon of chilli dipping sauce and add the chicken.

3   Put some baking paper on a baking tray and brush with oil. Now take out eight sheets of filo pastry. Place one sheet on a clean surface and dab it all over with oil. Place another piece on top. Dab this piece with oil too.

4   Turn the pastry with your hands so that a corner is pointing towards you (like a diamond). Spoon some of the filling onto the corner nearest you. Fold this corner towards the centre and tuck it under the filling. Fold the two outside corners in towards the middle so it looks like an envelope.

5   Dab with oil and then roll up the pastry to look like a sausage. Dab with more oil and put on the baking tray. Repeat until you have made four.

6   Ask an adult to place the baking tray in the preheated oven for 15–20 minutes until crisp and golden.

TOP TIP! Serve these scrummy spring rolls with sweet chilli dipping sauce!

TASTY TARTLETS

Ingredients:

- $1/2$ red onion, chopped
- 2 tomatoes, chopped
- 1 pepper, yellow or red, chopped
- 12 pre-bought cooked pastry cases
- basil leaves, to decorate

1 Ask an adult to help you wash and prepare the vegetables. Carefully cut them up into small chunks.

2 Fill the pastry cases, adding a selection of vegetables so each case gets a mixture.

3 Top with basil leaves to finish.

TOP TIP!
Why not add some cheese to the cases and ask an adult to place them under a grill for 2 minutes?

CHEESY PASTRIES

Ingredients:
- 100 g (3½ oz) butter, plus extra for greasing
- 150 g (5 oz) mature cheddar cheese, grated
- 100 g (3½ oz) plain flour, plus extra for dusting the work surface
- 1 egg yolk

1 Preheat the oven to 180°C / 350°F / gas mark 4.

2 Lightly grease a baking tray with butter and cover it with a piece of baking paper.

3 Put the cheese into a mixing bowl and sift in the flour. Next, cut the butter into little cubes and rub them into the mixture with your fingertips.

4 When you have a crumbly mixture, stir in the egg yolk.

5 Knead the mixture until it forms a dough. Then dust the work surface with plenty of flour. Roll out the dough into a square, until it is about 1 cm (½ in.) thick.

6 Ask an adult to cut the square into strips, then twist the strips or make them into circles or heart shapes. Gently lift them onto the baking tray.

7 Ask an adult to place the tray in a preheated oven and bake for about 8 minutes, until they are golden brown. Then, carefully transfer the pastries to a wire rack to cool.

TOP TIP!
For a tasty variation, add tomato pureé prior to twisting.

PASTRY POCKETS

MAKES 20

Ingredients:

• 375 g (13 oz) puff pastry

• 1 egg yolk (beaten with
  1 tablespoon water)

• 450 g (1 lb) favourite cheese

• 3 large tomatoes, sliced

• 3 teaspoons of sesame seeds

• basil, to decorate (optional)

1 Preheat the oven to 200°C / 400°F / gas mark 6.

2 Roll out the pastry so it is 0.5 cm (1/4 in.) thick. Cut into 8 cm (3 in.) squares and brush the edges with beaten egg.

3 Cut the cheese into 20 slices. Put a slice onto each piece of pastry, followed by a slice of tomato.

4 Pinch together the corners of the pastry and flatten slightly.

5 Place the pastry onto an oiled baking tray and brush with more beaten egg. Sprinkle with sesame seeds.

6 Bake for 15 minutes in the oven, until the pastry has puffed up. Serve warm or at room temperature, decorated with basil.

TOP TIP!
Why not cut the pastry into different shapes, such as stars or hearts, or if you're having a themed party, cut the shapes to reflect the theme!

MINI QUICHES

Ingredients:

- margarine, for greasing
- 1 pack of ready-made shortcrust pastry
- 2 eggs
- 150 ml (5 fl.oz) milk
- a pinch of herbs (optional)
- 50 g (2 oz) cheddar cheese, grated
- choice of fillings: tinned sweetcorn, chopped peppers, chopped cooked meat (ham, salami, chicken etc.), chopped mushrooms, frozen peas

1 Preheat the oven to 180°C / 350°F / gas mark 4.

2 Grease a bun tin with a little margarine. Next, roll the shortcrust pastry out until it is quite thin.

3 Cut out circles of pastry with the pastry cutter and then line the bun tin with the pastry circles. Re-roll any scraps to make more circles if needed.

4 Beat the eggs and milk together and then add the herbs (optional).

5 Place a little grated cheese in the bottom of each pastry case. Then add the fillings to each quiche.

6 Pour on the egg and milk mixture until it nearly reaches the top of the pastry.

7 Finally, ask an adult to place the bun tin in the preheated oven and bake for 15–25 minutes until lightly browned.

TOP TIP!
Prepare these quiches a day before to save time – they taste great cold.

PASTRY PARCELS

Ingredients:
- 4 sheets of pre-made filo pastry
- 200 g (7 oz) brie
- 4 tablespoons of olive oil
- 4 heaped teaspoons of cranberry sauce

1 Preheat the oven to 200°C / 400°F / gas mark 6.

2 Ask an adult to cut each piece of filo into four quarters and also to cut the brie into four.

3 To make a parcel, brush one of the pieces of filo pastry with olive oil. Put another piece over it to make a cross and brush with oil again. Lay a third piece diagonally, as if you were making a star shape, brush with oil, then top with the final piece, diagonally, to complete the 'star'. Brush with oil.

4 Place one of the pieces of brie in the centre of the pastry and put a heaped teaspoon of cranberry sauce on top of it.

5 Fold up the sides of the filo and scrunch them at the top so they hold together. Brush all over with olive oil. Make three more parcels in the same way.

6 Place all of the parcels on a lightly oiled baking sheet and bake in the oven for 15–20 minutes, or until crisp and lightly browned.

TOMATO & CHEESE TARTLETS

Ingredients:

For the tartlet cases:

- 225 g (8 oz) plain flour
- a pinch of salt
- 50 g (2 oz) butter
- 1-2 tablespoons cold water

For the tomato filling:

- 1 tablespoon olive oil
- 1 small onion, chopped finely
- 400 g (14 oz) tin of chopped tomatoes
- pinch dried oregano
- ½ teaspoon sugar

To finish the tartlets:

- 100 g (3½ oz) mozzarella cheese, thinly sliced
- 10 black olives, pitted and halved
- a little olive oil

1 Preheat the oven to 200°C / 400°F / gas mark 6.

2 Sift the flour and salt into a bowl and add the butter. Rub the butter with your fingers until the mixture resembles fine breadcrumbs.

3 Add enough water to make a smooth dough, kneading lightly. Cover with cling film and put into the fridge for 30 minutes. Roll out on a floured surface to 0.5 cm (¼ in.) thick. Use a cookie cutter to cut out circles of pastry and line tartlet trays. Leave in the fridge for 30 minutes.

4 Prick the base of each tartlet with a fork and bake in a preheated oven for 5 minutes. Cool and store in a container until needed.

5 To make the filling, ask an adult to put the oil into a small saucepan over a medium heat. Add the onion and cook gently for 4–5 minutes until soft. Add the tomatoes, oregano, and sugar. Cook for another 5–7 minutes, stirring occasionally until thick. Set aside to cool.

6 Put the pastry cases back into the tartlet trays and put a teaspoon of the mixture in each one. Put a piece of mozzarella cheese on top of each tartlet, followed by half an olive, if using. Brush with oil and bake in the oven for 5–7 minutes, until the cheese has melted. Serve warm!

OAT CRUNCH COOKIES

Ingredients:

- 100 g (3½ oz) butter
- 80 g (3 oz) demerara sugar
- 100 g (3½ oz) plain wholemeal flour
- 100 g (3½ oz) porridge oats

1. Preheat the oven to 180°C / 350°F / gas mark 4.

2. Cream the butter and sugar together in a bowl, until light. Add the flour and oats to the mixture and use your hands to create a soft dough.

3. Roll the dough out on a floured surface until 5 mm thick and cut into 25 rounds with a 5 cm (2 in.) cutter. Bake in the oven for 12–15 minutes or until cooked.

4. Transfer to a wire rack to cool. Store in an airtight container.

TOP TIP!
Try adding raisins to ring the changes with this recipe!

CRUNCHY APRICOT STICKS

Ingredients:

- 100 g (3½ oz) butter
- 100 g (3½ oz) brown sugar
- a few drops of vanilla extract
- 1 egg
- 80 g (3 oz) self-raising flour
- ½ teaspoon salt
- 80 g (3 oz) wheatgerm
- 50 g (2 oz) desiccated coconut
- 50 g (2 oz) rolled oats
- 100 g (3½ oz) dried apricots, chopped
- 50 g (2 oz) cornflakes
- 100 g (3½ oz) dark chocolate

1. Preheat the oven to 180°C / 350°F / gas mark 4.

2. Cream the butter, brown sugar, vanilla extract and egg together in a bowl.

3. Stir in the flour, salt, wheatgerm, coconut, rolled oats, chopped apricots and cornflakes and mix well.

4. Take one tablespoon of mixture, roll it gently in your hands to form a finger and place on a baking sheet lined with silicone paper. Flatten slightly to firm. Repeat with the rest of the mixture and ask an adult to bake for 10–12 minutes.

5. Leave to cool on wire racks.

6. Meanwhile, ask an adult to melt the chocolate in a bowl over a pan of boiling water.

7. Carefully dip the bases into the melted chocolate and drizzle some chocolate over the biscuits.

APRICOT & PISTACHIO BISCUITS

Ingredients:

- 50 g (2 oz) almond marzipan
- 80 g (3 oz) butter
- 2 teaspoons grated lime zest
- 1 tablespoon lime juice
- 50 g (2 oz) caster sugar
- 1 egg, separated
- 150 g (5 oz) plain flour
- 1 teaspoon water
- 50 g (2 oz) flaked almonds
- 25 g (1 oz) chopped pistachio nuts
- 50 g (2 oz) apricot jam

1 Preheat the oven to 180°C / 350°F / gas mark 4.

2 Combine the marzipan, butter, lime zest and juice, sugar and egg yolk in a large bowl.

3 Sift the flour into the mixture and knead gently until firm. Refrigerate for 20–30 minutes.

4 Roll the dough out on a floured surface until it is 1 cm (½ in.) thick, then cut into rounds with a 5 cm (2 in.) fluted cutter. Place on a baking sheet lined with baking paper.

5 Mix the egg white and water together and brush over the top of the biscuits before sprinkling with flaked almonds and chopped pistachios.

6 Ask an adult to bake for 10–15 minutes until pale golden brown.

7 Leave to cool, then brush with sieved apricot jam and return to the oven to glaze for 2–3 minutes. When cold, store in an airtight container.

COCONUT MACAROONS

Ingredients:
- 2 egg whites
- pinch of salt
- 150 g (5 oz) caster sugar
- 150 g (5 oz) desiccated coconut
- rice paper
- 10 glacé cherries, halved

1 Preheat the oven to 160°C / 320°F / gas mark 3.

2 In a bowl, whisk the egg whites with the salt, adding the sugar, a little at a time, until the mixture is stiff and forming peaks. Gently fold in the coconut.

3 Line a baking tray with rice paper and put 20 well spaced spoonfuls of the mixture onto the paper. Top each with half a glacé cherry. Ask an adult to bake for 25–30 minutes until firm.

4 Leave to cool on the rice paper. Tear or cut the paper around each macaroon when cool.

TOP TIP!
Make sure you use edible rice paper in this recipe!

APPLE & CINNAMON CUPCAKES

Ingredients:
- 190 g (7 oz) plain flour
- 100 g (3½ oz) butter, softened
- 125 g (4½ oz) caster sugar
- 2 eggs
- ½ teaspoon ground cinnamon
- ½ teaspoon ground allspice
- 2 teaspoons baking powder
- ½ teaspoon bicarbonate of soda
- 235 ml (8 fl.oz) apple sauce

For the topping:
- 200 g (8 oz) icing sugar
- 100 g (3½ oz) butter, softened
- a few drops of vanilla extract
- ½ teaspoon ground cinnamon

1 Preheat the oven to 180°C / 350°F / gas mark 4.

2 Sift the flour into a bowl. In another bowl, mix together the butter and sugar until the mixture is creamy.

3 Add in the eggs and beat until smooth. Blend in the cinnamon, allspice, baking powder and bicarbonate of soda.

4 Add the apple sauce and the sifted flour. Stir until just blended together.

5 Use a teaspoon to divide the mixture equally into bun cases. Bake the cupcakes for 10–15 minutes, until they are golden brown, then leave them to cool on a wire rack.

6 For the topping, sift the icing sugar into a bowl and then mix in the butter, vanilla extract and cinnamon. Add a little milk, if the mixture is too stiff, and then place in a piping bag.

7 Pipe the topping onto the cooled cupcakes and then finish with a light sprinkling of ground cinnamon.

TOP TIP!
Invest in a cake stand so you can show off your lovely cupcakes!

NUTTY CHOCOLATE FUDGE ✓

Ingredients:
- 300 g (10 oz) plain chocolate
- 200 ml (7 fl.oz) condensed milk
- 2 teaspoons vanilla extract
- 100 g (3½ oz) walnuts, chopped

1 Line a square baking tin with greaseproof paper.

2 Ask an adult to help you put the plain chocolate, condensed milk and vanilla extract into a saucepan over a medium heat. Stir them together until the chocolate has melted.

3 Add the chopped walnuts and stir until evenly combined.

4 Ask an adult to pour the mixture into the tin, and smooth the top with the back of a spoon. Put the tin into the fridge for 3–4 hours.

5 Remove the fudge from the tin by lifting it with the greaseproof paper. Turn it out onto a board and peel off the paper.

6 Cut the slab of fudge into squares and serve!

TOP TIP! Add white or dark chocolate to make different flavoured fudge!

WHITE CHOCOLATE & EXOTIC FRUIT COOKIES

Ingredients:

- 200 g (7 oz) plain flour
- 1 teaspoon baking powder
- 100 g (3½ oz) unsalted butter
- 100 g (3½ oz) light brown sugar
- 80 g (3 oz) white chocolate, chopped
- 80 g (3 oz) of mixed exotic dried fruit (papaya, pineapple, mango etc), chopped
- 1 teaspoon lemon zest
- 1 egg

1 Preheat the oven to 190°C / 375°F / gas mark 5. Line two baking trays with lightly greased baking parchment.

2 Sift the flour and baking powder into a bowl. Rub the butter into the flour with your fingertips.

3 Mix in the sugar, chopped chocolate and dried fruit.

4 Add the lemon zest and egg, plus a little extra water if necessary, and mix to form a soft dough.

5 Place spoonfuls of the mixture on the baking trays, leaving a space between each one.

6 Ask an adult to place the trays in the oven for 10–12 minutes until the cookies are a light, golden brown.

7 Allow to cool for 5 minutes, then transfer to a wire rack. Store in an airtight container.

TOP TIP!
Double the ingredients to make double the cookies!

34

STRAWBERRY GINGER SNAPS

Ingredients:
- 50 g (2 oz) butter
- 50 g (2 oz) caster sugar
- 50 g (2 oz) golden syrup
- 50 g (2 oz) flour
- ½ teaspoon ground ginger
- grated rind of half a lemon
- 1 tablespoon of lemon juice
- 300 ml (½ pt) double cream
- 15 g (½ oz) icing sugar
- 240 g (8½ oz) strawberries

1 Preheat the oven to 180°C / 350°F / gas mark 4.

2 Ask an adult to melt the butter, sugar and syrup in a small pan. Stir in the flour and ginger, add the grated lemon rind and the lemon juice.

3 Place 12 tablespoons of the mixture well spaced on baking parchment. Ask an adult to bake them in a preheated oven for 8–10 minutes until golden. Allow to cool slightly, and then slide off the paper onto a wire rack.

4 Ask an adult to whip the cream with the icing sugar until it forms soft peaks.

5 Spoon fresh cream into the middle of one ginger snap, surround with fresh strawberries and sandwich with a second ginger snap. Repeat with a third, and decorate the top with cream and a single strawberry.

6 Repeat the process to produce three more strawberry ginger snaps.

TOP TIP!
Why not try swapping the strawberries for other soft fruits?

CARROT CAKE

MAKES 12-15

Ingredients:

- 150 g (5 oz) self-raising flour
- 1 teaspoon baking powder
- 150 g (5 oz) soft brown sugar
- 50 g (2 oz) chopped walnuts
- 50 g (2 oz) raisins
- 100 g (3½ oz) grated carrots
- 2 eggs
- 150 ml (¼ pint) oil

For the topping:

- 50 g (2 oz) icing sugar
- 75 g (3 oz) cream cheese
- a few drops of vanilla extract
- chopped walnuts to decorate

1 Preheat the oven to 180°C / 350°F / gas mark 4.

2 Put a square baking tin on a sheet of greaseproof paper. Draw around it and cut out the shape. Grease the tin with a little margarine. Then place the greaseproof paper inside.

3 Sift the flour and baking powder into a bowl. Add the sugar, nuts, raisins and carrots and stir them together well.

4 Add the eggs and oil to the bowl. Beat all the ingredients together until they are well mixed.

5 Spoon the mixture into the prepared tin, spreading it into the corners, and smooth the top carefully with a spoon.

6 Bake the cake for one hour, or until it is firm to the touch.

7 To make the topping, mix the icing sugar, cream cheese and vanilla extract together.

8 Spread the topping mixture over the cake and sprinkle it with chopped walnuts. Keep the cake in the fridge until you are ready to serve it.

BLUEBERRY MUFFINS ✓

Ingredients:
- 50 g (2 oz) butter
- 2 eggs
- 200 g (7 oz) sugar
- 250 g (9 oz) plain flour
- 2 teaspoons baking powder
- 100 ml (4 fl.oz) milk
- a few drops of vanilla extract
- 300 g (10 oz) blueberries

1 Preheat the oven to 180°C / 350°F / gas mark 4.

2 Place paper muffin cases into a muffin tray.

3 Add the butter, eggs and sugar to a large bowl. Beat them until well mixed.

4 Mix the flour with the baking powder and sift into the first mixture, alternating with the milk.

5 Blend in the vanilla extract and add the blueberries. Mix everything together until just moistened.

6 Use a teaspoon to divide the mixture equally into the muffin tray. Bake the muffins for 30 minutes or until golden brown.

7 Leave the muffins in the tray until they are cool, and then turn out and enjoy.

TOP TIP! Muffins are best enjoyed warm. Leftover muffins can be reheated for a few minutes in the oven the next day.

CRANBERRY ORANGE CAKES

Ingredients:

- 250 g (9 oz) plain flour
- 150 g (5 oz) sugar
- 1 tablespoon baking powder
- 1 egg
- 175 ml (6 fl.oz) milk
- 3 tablespoons vegetable oil
- 75 g (3 oz) chopped cranberries
- 2 tablespoons grated orange peel
- 2 tablespoons chopped pecans
  or walnuts

1 Preheat the oven to 190°C / 375°F / gas mark 5.

2 Place paper muffin cases into a muffin tray.

3 Sift the flour, sugar and baking powder into a bowl. Mix them together.

4 Add in the egg, milk and vegetable oil and mix until all the flour is moistened.

5 Fold in the cranberries, orange peel and nuts.

6 Use a teaspoon to transfer equal amounts of the mixture to the paper cases. Bake the muffins for 20 minutes or until they are well risen and golden brown. Leave them to cool on a wire rack.

WHITE CHOCOLATE CAKE

Ingredients:
- 200 g (7 oz) butter, softened
- 200 g (7 oz) golden caster sugar
- 200 g (7 oz) self-raising flour
- 50 g (2 oz) ground almonds
- 2 eggs, beaten
- 2 egg yolks, beaten
- 2 tablespoons milk

For the filling:
- 600 g (1 lb 5 oz) mascarpone
- 50 ml (2 fl.oz) milk
- 175 g (6 oz) icing sugar, sifted
- grated zest and juice of 2 limes
- 75 g (3 oz) white chocolate, grated

1 Preheat the oven to 160°C / 325°F / gas mark 3. Line the base of two sandwich tins with baking parchment.

2 Put all of the sponge ingredients in a bowl, then beat until creamy and well mixed.

3 Divide the mixture between the two sandwich tins and level the tops with a spoon or spatula.

4 Bake both cakes for about 40 minutes or until golden brown. (Use a knife to check that your sponge is cooked in the middle. If the knife comes out clean, then your cake is ready.) Ask an adult to remove the cakes from the tins and cool on a wire rack.

5 Place all of the ingredients for the cream filling into a bowl and mix well. Refrigerate for 30 minutes before using.

6 Spread the filling onto the top of one of the sponges with a spatula and place the other sponge on top. Continue spreading the filling over the top and sides of the cake to finish.

TOP TIP!
Make sure your cakes are completely cool before filling.

WELSH CAKES

Ingredients:

- 225 g (8 oz) self-raising flour
- 110 g (4 oz) salted butter, softened
- 85 g (3 oz) caster sugar
- handful of sultanas
- 1 egg
- milk, if needed
- extra butter, for greasing
- extra caster sugar, for dusting

1 Sieve the flour into a bowl and add the butter. Use your hands to mix the butter into the flour until the mixture resembles breadcrumbs.

2 Mix in the sugar, sultanas and egg until it forms a ball of dough. Add a splash of milk if the mixture is too dry.

3 Roll out the mixture until it is about 0.5 cm (1/4 in.) thick. Then, use the cookie cutter to cut out circles of dough.

4 Ask an adult to grease a griddle or frying pan with a little butter and place on the heat.

5 Once hot, place the Welsh cakes on the griddle, turning once. Each Welsh cake should take about 2–3 minutes per side – it should be caramel brown before turning.

6 Remove from the pan and dust with caster sugar while still warm.

TOP TIP
Replace the sultanas with chocolate chips for a chocolatey treat.

SHORTBREAD

Ingredients:

- 130 g (4$\frac{1}{2}$ oz) butter, softened
- 60 g (2$\frac{1}{2}$ oz) caster sugar, plus extra for sprinkling
- 130 g (4$\frac{1}{2}$ oz) plain flour
- 60 g (2$\frac{1}{2}$ oz) rice flour
- pinch of salt

1 Preheat the oven to 170°C / 325°F / gas mark 3.

2 Cream the butter and sugar together in a large bowl, until pale and fluffy.

3 Sift in both flours and the salt and mix well.

4 Use your hands to bring the mixture together and press it into a cake tin. Smooth the top with the back of a spoon. Score the mixture into eight pieces with a knife and prick each piece with a fork. Use your thumb to indent around the edge of the shortbread.

5 Put the mixture in the refrigerator for 30 minutes to firm.

6 Remove the shortbread from the refrigerator and bake for 30–35 minutes, or until pale golden-brown.

7 Ask an adult to remove the shortbread from the oven and sprinkle with a little caster sugar.

8 Leave the shortbread to cool in the tin for a few minutes. Then, remove it from the tin and leave to cool completely on a wire rack.

9 Cut the shortbread into eight pieces, along the scored lines, and enjoy!

TOP TIP!
Keep the shortbread in an airtight container to prevent it from going soft.

CLASSIC SCONES

Ingredients:

- 225 g (8 oz) self-raising flour
- 1 teaspoon baking powder
- pinch of salt
- 25 g (1 oz) caster sugar
- 50 g (2 oz) unsalted butter, softened
- 150 ml (5 fl.oz) milk
- 1 egg, beaten
- clotted cream, to serve
- jam, to serve

1 Preheat the oven to 220°C / 425°F / gas mark 7. Grease a baking tray with a little butter.

2 Sift together the flour, baking powder and salt into a bowl. Stir in the sugar.

3 Add the butter and rub it into the flour mixture until it resembles fine breadcrumbs.

4 Add the milk, a little at a time, until it becomes a smooth dough.

5 Lightly flour the work surface and then roll out the dough until it is about 2 cm (3/4 in.) thick.

6 Use the pastry cutter to cut the dough into round scones. Re-roll any dough that is left over and cut out more scones. Place onto the baking tray.

7 Brush the tops of the scones with the beaten egg. Ask an adult to place in the oven and bake for 10–12 minutes, or until golden brown.

8 Serve with clotted cream and jam.

TOP TIP! Why not try making fruit scones by adding 50 g (2 oz) raisins or sultanas to the dry ingredients?

MIXED BERRY SORBET

Ingredients:
- 100 g (3½ oz) caster sugar
- 180 ml (6 fl.oz) water
- 2 teaspoons glucose syrup
- 450 g (1 lb) mixed berries, (fresh or frozen), reserving some for decoration
- squeeze of lemon juice
- sugar sprinkles, to decorate

1 Pour the sugar, 100 ml (3 fl.oz) of the water and the glucose syrup into a saucepan. Ask an adult to dissolve the sugar over a medium heat without stirring. Bring to the boil and simmer briskly for 5–7 minutes until the mixture thickens to a syrup. Remove from the heat, pour into a bowl and leave to cool.

2 Put the mixed berries in another saucepan. Squeeze some lemon juice over them and simmer over a low heat for a minute or two until soft.

3 Put the mixed berries in a blender and ask an adult to whizz until smooth. Then, push the purée through a fine sieve to remove all of the seeds.

4 Add the cooled syrup and remaining water to the purée and whisk together.

5 Pour the mixture into an ice cream maker and churn until frozen. Alternatively, if you don't have an ice cream maker you can freeze your sorbet in a plastic tub in a freezer.

6 Once frozen, scoop into a glass. Garnish with some leftover berries, some sugar sprinkles and a cool cocktail decoration.

TOP TIP!
A great teatime treat for a hot summer's day!

ORANGE SORBET

Ingredients:
- 500 ml (17 fl.oz) water
- 200 g (7 oz) caster sugar
- 4 large oranges
- 2 tablespoons orange juice

1 Ask an adult to heat the water and sugar in a saucepan, being careful not to boil the mixture. Stir for 2 minutes until the mixture is syrup-like in consistency, then transfer to a bowl to cool.

2 Grate the rind from two of the oranges and squeeze the juice from four, reserving four halved orange skins for later. Mix the juice and rind in a bowl, then stir the extra orange juice into the cooled sugar syrup, followed by the juice and rind mixture.

3 Cover, then leave to chill in the fridge for an hour.

4 Next, pour the mixture into an ice cream maker and churn until frozen. Alternatively, if you don't have an ice cream maker you can freeze the sorbet in a plastic tub in a freezer.

5 Once frozen, scoop the sorbet into the reserved orange halves. Garnish with a few rind ribbons (ask an adult to grate these) to finish.

TOP TIP!
Presenting sorbets in their skins looks great! You could try making a lemon sorbet too!

44

CHOCOLATE TRUFFLES

Ingredients:
• 150 g (6 oz) plain chocolate
• 150 ml (5 fl.oz) double cream
• 25 g (1 oz) butter

To coat the truffles:
• cocoa powder
• chocolate strands
• chopped nuts

1 Ask an adult to put a heatproof bowl over a saucepan of just-simmering water, making sure the bowl doesn't touch the water. Break the plain chocolate into small pieces and put it into the bowl, and then add the cream and butter. Stir the mixture until the chocolate has melted.

2 Take the saucepan off the heat. Take the bowl off the saucepan and leave it to cool for a few minutes. Carefully pour the melted chocolate into a plastic container. Put the lid on the container and leave it in the fridge to set for 3–4 hours.

3 Remove the container from the fridge. Roll small balls of the chocolate truffle mixture in your hands.

4 Roll the balls in cocoa powder, chocolate strands or chopped nuts, and then put them into sweet cases.

5 Store the truffles in a container in the fridge until you're ready to eat them or give them as a gift.

TOP TIP!
You'll have to roll the truffle balls quickly or the mixture will melt in your hands!

LEMON WHOOPIE PIES

Ingredients:
- 75 g (3 oz) unsalted butter, softened
- 150 g (5 oz) caster sugar
- 1 large egg, beaten
- 2 tablespoons fresh lemon juice
- 2 teaspoons lemon zest, finely grated
- 275 g (10 oz) plain flour
- 3/4 teaspoon bicarbonate of soda
- 1/8 teaspoon salt
- 145 ml (5 fl.oz) buttermilk

For the filling:
- 50 g (2 oz) unsalted butter
- 300 g (10 1/2 oz) icing sugar
- 125 g (4 1/2 oz) cream cheese
- 2 tablespoons fresh lemon juice

1 Grease a whoopie pie tray with a little butter. Preheat the oven to 180°C / 350°F / gas mark 4.

2 Soften the butter then cream with the sugar in a bowl until light and fluffy. Gradually add the egg, lemon juice and zest.

3 Sift the flour, bicarbonate of soda and salt together in another bowl.

4 Gradually add a third of the dry ingredients to the mixture, followed by a third of the buttermilk. Continue adding alternately, and mixing to form a thick, smooth cake mixture.

5 Use a piping bag or a tablespoon to transfer the mixture onto the tray.

6 Ask an adult to bake in the oven for 12–14 minutes until risen and firm to the touch. Cool for 5 minutes in the trays before transferring to a wire rack.

For the filling:

7 Ask an adult to beat the butter and icing sugar together for a few minutes using a whisk or electric mixer.

8 Add the cream cheese and beat together until the filling is light and fluffy. Finally, add the lemon juice and mix.

9 Using either a piping bag or a spoon, spread the filling evenly over one half of the whoopie pie and sandwich together with the second half.

COURGETTE & CHOCOLATE LOAF

Ingredients:

- 175 g (6 oz) butter, softened
- 150 g (5 oz) soft brown sugar
- 3 eggs, beaten
- 1 medium courgette, grated
- 50 g (2 oz) chocolate chips
- 50 g (2 oz) marzipan, finely chopped
- 175 g (6 oz) self-raising flour
- 50 g (2 oz) cocoa powder

1 Preheat the oven to 180°C / 350°F / gas mark 4.

2 Grease a 1 kg (2 lb) loaf tin with a little butter.

3 Cream the butter and sugar together until the mixture is fluffy and pale, then add the beaten eggs, one at a time. Mix well.

4 Now add the grated courgette, chocolate chips and chopped marzipan, and mix.

5 Sift together the flour and cocoa powder, and fold into the mixture.

6 Transfer the mixture to the loaf tin and bake for 50–55 minutes or until firm to the touch.

7 Allow the loaf to cool for 15 minutes, then serve warm.

TOP TIP!
Set a timer so you don't forget about your loaf in the oven!

47

CHOCOLATE POTS

SERVES 6

Ingredients:

- 2 eggs
- 2 egg yolks
- 15 g (½ oz) caster sugar
- 1 teaspoon cornflour
- 570 ml (1 pt) milk
- 100 g (3½ oz) dark chocolate
- 4 tablespoons chocolate and hazelnut spread
- 100 ml (3 fl.oz) whipping cream, beaten until stiff

1 Beat together the two eggs, egg yolks, sugar and cornflour until well mixed.

2 Ask an adult to heat the milk until nearly boiling. Gradually pour the hot milk onto the egg mixture whilst whisking.

3 Heat the dark chocolate and hazelnut spread in a bowl over warm water. When melted, whisk into the egg mixture.

4 Grease six small ramekins or ovenproof dishes and pour equal portions of the mixture into each one. Cover the tops with foil and place in a roasting tray. Fill the tray with water halfway up the dishes, and place in a preheated oven at 160°C / 325°F / gas mark 3 for 30–40 minutes, or until the mixture sets.

5 Remove the ramekins from the tray and chill until required. Decorate the tops with whipped cream.

TOP TIP!
Make sure that the eggs used are very fresh and preferably free-range as this will improve the taste.

VANILLA CUPCAKES

Ingredients:
- 225 g (8 oz) self-raising flour
- 80 g (3 oz) butter
- 80 g (3 oz) caster sugar
- 1 egg
- 80–100 ml (3–4 fl.oz) milk

For the topping:
- 200 g (8 oz) icing sugar
- 100 g (4 oz) butter, softened
- 1 teaspoon vanilla extract
- 1 tablespoon milk
- sugar sprinkles

1. Preheat the oven to 180°C / 350°F / gas mark 4.

2. Sift the flour into a bowl, followed by the butter.

3. Use the tips of your fingers to rub the butter and flour together until the mixture becomes crumbly.

4. Add the sugar and mix it in, then stir in the egg. Finally, add enough milk to make the mixture creamy.

5. Put spoonfuls of the mixture into bun cases. Bake the buns for 10–15 minutes, until they are golden brown, then leave them to cool on a wire rack.

6. Sift the icing sugar into a bowl and then add the butter, vanilla extract and a tablespoon of milk. Mix well. Then place the mixture into a piping bag.

7. Pipe the topping onto the cooked cupcakes and then finish with sugar sprinkles.

TOP TIP!
Serve your cupcakes in saucers for a posh teatime twist!

BRAZILIAN BRIGADEIRO

Ingredients:
- 200 g (7 oz) sweetened condensed milk
- 1/2 tablespoon butter
- 1 1/2 tablespoons cocoa powder
- 1/2 teaspoon vanilla extract
- dark chocolate sprinkles, to cover

1 Ask an adult to put the condensed milk, butter and cocoa powder into a saucepan over a medium heat.

2 Stir the mixture constantly, until it thickens enough to show the bottom of the pan when stirring, after about 10 minutes.

3 Remove the mixture from the heat and stir in the vanilla extract.

4 Grease a baking tin with butter and ask an adult to pour the mixture into the tin. Let the mixture cool to room temperature.

5 Grease your hands with a little butter and then take teaspoonfuls of the mixture and roll into small balls.

6 Roll each ball in the chocolate sprinkles until completely covered.

7 Place in mini paper cases and enjoy!

TOP TIP!
If the balls don't hold their shape, cook for another 5 minutes until the mixture thickens further.

CHOCOLATE APPLES

Ingredients:
- 12 dessert apples, peeled
- 1 kg (2 lb 2 oz) milk chocolate, chopped

For the topping:
- sugar sprinkles
- chopped nuts
- melted chocolate

1 Ask an adult to insert wooden sticks into the cores of the apples at the stem.

2 Next, ask an adult to put a heatproof bowl over a saucepan of just-simmering water. Make sure the bowl doesn't touch the water. Break the chocolate into small pieces and put them in the bowl. Stir until the chocolate has melted, then remove from the heat.

3 Next, dip the peeled apples into the melted chocolate, turning to coat completely.

4 Then, dip or roll the apples in your selected topping, and place on a sheet of greaseproof paper. Repeat with the remaining apples.

5 Allow the chocolate covering to set at room temperature. Check to make sure it is firm before serving.

TOP TIP!
Experiment with the toppings and also the chocolate. Why not try white or dark?

CHOCOLATE PINWHEEL COOKIES

Ingredients:
- 200 g (7 oz) unsalted butter
- 150 g (5 oz) caster sugar
- 2 teaspoons vanilla extract
- 1 egg
- 300 g (10 oz) plain flour, sifted
- 25 g (1 oz) cocoa powder

1 Preheat the oven to 180°C / 350°F / gas mark 4.

2 Put the butter and sugar in a bowl and mix together well. Next, beat in the vanilla and egg, then add the flour. Knead until a dough forms, then remove from the bowl.

3 Halve the dough and fold the cocoa powder thoroughly into one portion.

4 Shape both dough portions into rough oblong shapes, then wrap in cling film and put in the refrigerator for 30 minutes to chill until firm.

5 Once firm, roll out each dough portion, trying to maintain the oblong shape.

6 Put the chocolate dough on top of the vanilla dough and ask an adult to trim the edges to neaten. Roll up lengthways, then wrap in cling film and chill again for 45 minutes.

7 Ask an adult to slice the dough into discs, then put them on a baking tray, spacing them out evenly. Cook for 15 minutes, then turn out to cool on a wire rack.

TOP TIP!
Serve these delicious cookies with vanilla ice cream!

CHOCOLATE FLORENTINES

MAKES 20

Ingredients:
- 60 ml (2 fl.oz) milk
- 75 g (3 oz) butter
- 100 g (3½ oz) icing sugar
- 50 g (2 oz) plain flour
- 50 g (2 oz) chopped nuts
- 50 g (2 oz) flaked almonds

For the chocolate coating:
- 100 g (3½ oz) dark, milk or white chocolate
- 10 g (⅓ oz) unsalted butter

1. Preheat the oven to 190°C / 375°F / gas mark 4. Line two baking trays with greaseproof paper.

2. In a saucepan, ask an adult to heat the milk, butter and icing sugar, stirring until the sugar has dissolved.

3. Off the heat, add the plain flour, chopped nuts and flaked almonds. Allow the mixture to go cold.

4. Spoon small quantities of the mixture onto the baking trays. Allow plenty of space between them as the mixture spreads when it is cooking.

5. Cook for about 7–10 minutes until golden brown.

6. Leave to cool for 10 minutes, then carefully transfer to a wire cooling rack.

7. Ask an adult to put a heatproof bowl over a saucepan of just-simmering water. Make sure the bowl doesn't touch the water. Add the chocolate and butter and stir until they have melted. Melt a different type of chocolate in a separate bowl if you wish.

8. Dip each florentine into the chocolate so the base and sides are covered in the chocolate mixture. Allow them to cool completely, chocolate side up.

TOP TIP!
Why not add some candied fruit for a fruity alternative to nuts?

GARDEN CUPCAKES

MAKES 12-15

Ingredients:
- 3 eggs, beaten
- 150 g (5 oz) butter, softened
- 150 g (5 oz) sugar
- 175 g (6 oz) self-raising flour
- a few drops of vanilla extract
- 2 drops green food colouring

For the topping:
- 150 g (5 oz) butter, softened
- 250 g (9 oz) icing sugar
- a few drops of vanilla extract
- 2 drops green food colouring
- 2 teaspoons hot water
- edible flowers, to decorate

1 Preheat the oven to 190°C / 375°F / gas mark 5.

2 Crack the eggs into a bowl and beat lightly with a fork.

3 Place the butter, sugar, flour (sifted) and vanilla extract into a large bowl. Add the beaten eggs and a couple of drops of green food colouring.

4 Beat until the mixture is light and creamy.

5 Use a teaspoon to transfer equal amounts of the mixture into bun cases. Bake the cupcakes for 18–20 minutes. Leave them to cool on a wire rack.

6 For the topping, beat together the butter and icing sugar. Once well mixed, add the vanilla extract, food colouring and water. Beat the mixture until smooth and creamy.

7 Swirl over your cupcakes and decorate with edible flowers.

TOP TIP! If you use real flowers, remember to remove them before eating!

MINI CHOCOLATE MERINGUES

Ingredients:
- 3 egg whites
- 150 g (5 oz) caster sugar
- 50 g (2 oz) dark chocolate, grated
- 2 teaspoons cocoa powder

1 Preheat the oven to 140°C / 275°F / gas mark 1.

2 Line two baking trays with greaseproof paper.

3 Next, whisk three egg whites until soft peaks form, then gradually whisk in the caster sugar until stiff peaks form.

4 Stir together the dark chocolate and sifted cocoa powder and fold gently into the meringue mixture.

5 Place the mixture into a piping bag and squeeze 3.5 cm (1 1/2 in) 'blobs' of the mixture onto the baking trays and ask an adult to quickly place them into the oven for 40 minutes.

6 Once cool, dust with cocoa powder, and serve.

TOP TIP!
To separate the egg white from the yolk, crack the egg lightly, then hold half the shell, with the yolk in it, in one hand, and the other half-shell in the other. Allow as much of the egg white as possible to run out of the shell and down into a bowl, then transfer the yolk to the other half of the shell, allowing more of the white to run out.

MACARONS

Ingredients:
- 175 g (6 oz) icing sugar
- 125 g (4½ oz) ground almonds
- 3 egg whites
- pinch of salt
- 75 g (2½ oz) caster sugar
- food colouring

For the filling:
- 150 g (5¼ oz) butter, softened
- 75 g (2½ oz) icing sugar
- food colouring (optional)

1 Preheat the oven to 160°C / 320°F / gas mark 3. Line two baking trays with baking paper.

2 Place the icing sugar and ground almonds in a food processor and blend to a very fine mixture, then sift into a bowl.

3 In a separate bowl, whisk the egg whites with a pinch of salt to form soft peaks, then gradually whisk in the caster sugar until the mixture is thick and glossy. Add a few drops of food colouring. If you want, separate the mixture into batches and colour each individually.

4 Fold half the almond and icing sugar mixture into the meringue and mix well. Mix in the rest until shiny and thick.

5 Spoon the mixture into a piping bag fitted with a 1 cm (½ in.) plain nozzle. Pipe small rounds of the macaron mixture, about 3 cm (1 in.) across, onto the baking trays.

6 Leave the macarons to stand at room temperature for 10–15 minutes to form a slight skin. Place in the oven and bake for 15 minutes. Remove from the oven and cool.

7 For the filling, beat the butter until light and fluffy, then beat in the icing sugar. Add a few drops of food colouring to match the macarons (optional).

8 Spread the filling onto the cooled macarons and sandwich together.

CHOCOLATE-CHIP CHEESECAKE

SERVES 12

Ingredients:
- 125 g (4½ oz) digestive biscuits
- 5 tablespoons caster sugar
- 75 g (3 oz) butter, melted
- 5 tablespoons unsweetened cocoa powder

For the filling:
- 675 g (1 lb 5 oz) cream cheese
- 397 g (14 oz) tin condensed milk
- 2 teaspoons vanilla extract
- 3 eggs
- 120 g (4½ oz) chocolate chips
- 1 teaspoon plain flour

To decorate:
- chocolate wafer stick
- runny honey

1 Preheat the oven to 150°C / 300°F / gas mark 2.

2 Place the biscuits in a strong plastic bag and crush them into fine crumbs with a rolling pin.

3 Then, mix the crumbs, sugar, butter and cocoa powder together in a bowl. Press onto the bottom and up the sides of a springform cake tin.

4 To make the filling, put the cream cheese into a bowl, then gradually add the condensed milk, beating well.

5 Next, add the vanilla extract and the eggs, and beat again until smooth.

6 Add the chocolate chips, along with the flour (this keeps them from sinking to the bottom of the cheesecake) and mix well. Pour over the prepared biscuit base.

7 Ask an adult to place in the oven and bake for 1 hour. After an hour, turn off the oven (do not open the oven door) and leave the cake to cool for another hour. Then remove from the oven and cool completely.

8 Refrigerate before removing the sides of the tin. When you're ready to serve, drizzle honey over the top of the cheesecake and top with a chocolate wafer stick.

CARAMEL NUT SWEETS

Ingredients:

- 50 g (1¾ oz) granulated sugar
- 50 g (1¾ oz) brown sugar
- 85 ml (3 fl.oz) golden syrup
- 55 g (2 oz) butter
- 120 ml (4 fl.oz) double cream
- ½ teaspoon vanilla extract
- mixed nuts, to decorate
- dried fruit, to decorate

1 Ask an adult to put both sugars, golden syrup, butter and half of the cream into a saucepan. Bring the mixture to the boil, stirring often and then stir in the rest of the cream.

2 Heat without stirring until the mixture begins to change colour. When the mixture is ready you should be able to drop a small amount into cold water and it will form a firm ball (ask an adult to do this using a teaspoon).

3 Remove the mixture from the heat and stir in the vanilla extract.

4 Allow the mixture to cool a little, then spoon into sweet cases.

5 Place a few mixed nuts and some dried fruit on top of each sweet to finish.

6 Place in the refrigerator to set.

58

CHOCOLATE MACARONS

MAKES 18-20

Ingredients:
- 140 g (5 oz) ground almonds
- 275 g (9½ oz) icing sugar
- 25 g (1 oz) cocoa powder
- 4 egg whites

For the filling:
- chocolate spread

1. Preheat the oven to 180°C / 350°F / gas mark 4.

2. First, blend the almonds, icing sugar and cocoa powder until very fine. Ask an adult for help with the blender.

3. Next, in a clean bowl, whisk the egg whites until stiff peaks form and then fold into the almond mixture.

4. Then, place into a piping bag and pipe circles onto a baking tray lined with baking parchment. Leave to set for 15 minutes.

5. Place in the oven to bake for 7–8 minutes. Then, remove the macarons from the parchment to cool (see top tip).

6. Once cool, spread the chocolate spread filling onto one macaron, then sandwich with another macaron.

7. Repeat with all of the macarons until they are all used up.

TOP TIP!
To remove the macarons without them sticking or tearing, ask an adult to lift one corner of the parchment and pour boiled water onto the tray. As the water hits the base of the parchment the macarons will lift off easily.

CHOCOLATE MOUSSE

Ingredients:
- 200 g (7 oz) good-quality dark chocolate, broken into pieces
- 30 ml (1 fl.oz) milk
- 1 teaspoon dark-roast coffee granules
- 5 very fresh free-range eggs, separated
- 50 g (2 oz) grated dark chocolate, to decorate

1 Ask an adult to put the dark chocolate and the milk in a heatproof bowl over a saucepan of barely simmering water. Stir them occasionally.

2 As soon as the chocolate pieces have melted, stir in the coffee granules and ask an adult to immediately remove the pan from the heat.

3 Allow the mixture to cool completely, then stir in the beaten egg yolks.

4 In a clean bowl, beat the egg whites until they form stiff peaks.

5 Gradually and carefully fold the beaten egg whites into the chocolate mixture, a spoonful at a time. Continue until all the egg whites have been used.

6 Spoon the mousse into attractive glasses and refrigerate for 3 hours. Before serving, sprinkle each mousse with grated dark chocolate.

TOP TIP!
Add fresh strawberries to this sweet teatime treat!

ICE CREAM BON BONS

Ingredients:
• 200 g (7 oz) dark chocolate
• 100 g (3½ oz) almonds, chopped
• 500 ml (17 fl.oz) vanilla ice cream

1 Cover a baking tray with greaseproof paper.

2 Ask an adult to put a heatproof bowl over a saucepan of just simmering water, making sure the bowl doesn't touch the water. Break the chocolate into small pieces and put them in the bowl.

3 Stir until the chocolate has melted and then mix in the almonds thoroughly.

4 Take the chocolate off the heat and allow to cool to just before it stiffens again.

5 Scoop the ice cream into small, round balls. Use a melon baller if you have one.

6 Dip each ice cream ball into the cooled chocolate mixture.

7 Place on a baking tray and put in the freezer to set the chocolate.

TOP TIP!
Experiment with the ice cream flavour, chocolate and nuts until you find your perfect combination!

FLOWER PETAL CUPCAKES

TOP TIP!
Make smaller petals and flowers so you can add more than one to each cake!

Ingredients:
- 125 g (4^1/$_2$ oz) self-raising flour
- 125 g (4^1/$_2$ oz) butter, softened
- 125 g (4^1/$_2$ oz) caster sugar
- 2 eggs
- a few drops of vanilla extract
- 2–3 tablespoons milk

For the topping:
- 140 g (5 oz) butter, softened
- 280 g (10 oz) icing sugar
- 1–2 tablespoons milk
- a few drops of pink food colouring
- ready-to-roll icing
- sweets, to decorate

1 Preheat the oven to 180°C / 350°F / gas mark 4.

2 Sift the flour into a bowl, followed by the butter. Use your fingertips to rub the butter and flour together until the mixture becomes crumbly. Add the sugar and mix it in, then stir in the eggs. Finally, add the vanilla extract and milk to make the mixture creamy.

3 Put spoonfuls of the mixture into bun cases. Bake the cupcakes for 10–15 minutes, until they are golden brown, then leave them to cool on a wire rack.

4 For the topping, place the butter in a large bowl and add half of the icing sugar. Beat until smooth.

5 Add the remaining icing sugar and 1 tablespoon of milk and beat the mixture until creamy and smooth. Beat in more milk if necessary to loosen the icing. Place in a piping bag and pipe on top of the cupcakes.

6 Next, knead a few drops of food colouring (more or less depending on how pink you would like the petals to be) into a section of the ready-to-roll icing. Once the colour is even, roll out the icing. Ask an adult to cut the icing into petal shapes, using a sharp knife. Run the knife lightly over each petal to add texture. Form the petals together so they make a flower and curl the outside of the petals upwards. Place the petals onto each cupcake and top with a sweet.

CHOCOLATE MESS CUPCAKES

Ingredients:
- 100 g (3½ oz) self-raising flour
- 1 tablespoon cocoa powder
- 125 g (4 ½ oz) butter, softened
- 125 g (4 ½ oz) caster sugar
- 2 large eggs
- 2–3 tablespoons milk
- 50 g (2 oz) chocolate chips

For the topping:
- 200 g (7 oz) dark chocolate
- 25 g (1 oz) butter
- 2 tablespoons double cream
- milk chocolate, grated

1 Preheat the oven to 180°C / 350°F / gas mark 4.

2 Sift the flour and cocoa powder into a bowl.

3 Put the butter in the bowl. Use the tips of your fingers to rub the butter, flour and cocoa powder together until the mixture becomes crumbly.

4 Add the sugar and mix it in, then stir in the eggs.

5 Finally, add the milk to make the mixture creamy, followed by the chocolate chips.

6 Put spoonfuls of the mixture into bun cases. Bake the cupcakes for 10–15 minutes, then leave them to cool on a wire rack.

7 For the topping, ask an adult to help you put some water in a saucepan over a medium heat. Put the chocolate, butter and cream in a heatproof bowl on top, making sure the bowl doesn't touch the water. Melt the ingredients, stirring the mixture with a wooden spoon.

8 Spoon the melted chocolate on top of each cupcake and leave to set. Once cool, top with grated milk chocolate.

TOP TIP!
Don't worry if these cupcakes look messy – that's what they're all about!

INDEX OF RECIPES

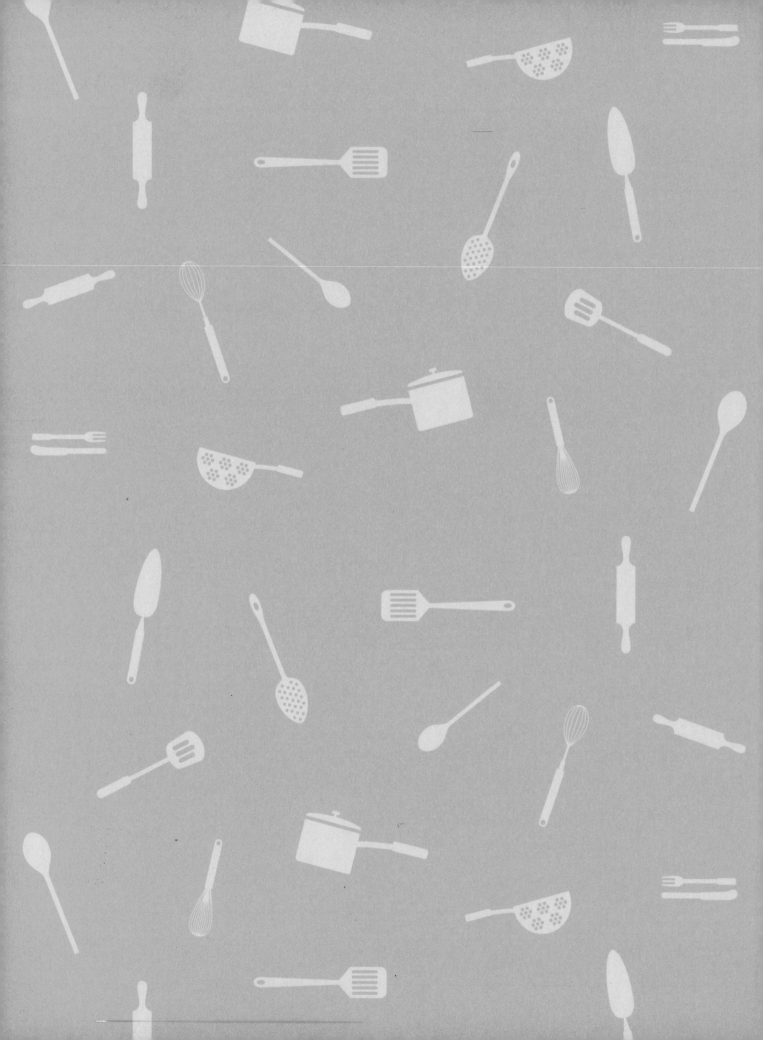